Caring for Myself

A Social Skills Storybook

Christy Gast and Jane Krug

Photography by Kotoe Laackman

Jessica Kingsley Publishers
London and Philadelphia

To Alec, Bobby, Charlie, Emma, Katie, Lillian, Ryan, and Sophia
– may you always know how special you are!

First published in 2008
by Jessica Kingsley Publishers
116 Pentonville Road
London N1 9JB, UK
and
400 Market Street, Suite 400
Philadelphia, PA 19106, USA

www.jkp.com

Copyright © Christy Gast and Jane Krug 2008
Photographs copyright © Kotoe Laackman 2008

Library of Congress Cataloging in Publication Data
A CIP catalog record for this book is available from the Library of Congress

British Library Cataloguing in Publication Data
A CIP catalogue record for this book is available from the British Library

ISBN 978 1 84310 872 6

Printed and bound in the People's Republic of China

Contents

Acknowledgments

We would like to acknowledge the many people who supported and helped us complete this book. First, we'd like to extend our thank you to the children who were photographed throughout the book. All were a joy to work with and personalities became apparent in each story! A special thank you to the parents of the children photographed in each story. We appreciate you sharing your children with us. Some of these parents agreed to be photographed as well, and we thank you for your participation. We'd also like to thank the Aurora Hair Salon and Forest Hills Pediatrics for so graciously agreeing to have photos taken at your place of business. Specifically, we'd like to thank Nancy Morgan, Dr. Richard Wood, Brenda Kain, and Leigh Hunt. The Gray Center for Social Learning and Understanding, especially Laurel, has been instrumental in supporting us through this project and we thank each staff member for your encouragement. Most importantly, thank you to our families. Your support, flexibility, and patience throughout this journey has been and continues to be amazing. Last but not least, our talented photographer Kotoe Laackman has gone above and beyond our expectations. We sincerely thank her for her time, effort, and incredible ability in helping this book come together with such beautiful images!

Introduction

This book was created for children who need extra support and guidance in understanding routines related to caring for their bodies. Through attention to word, sentence, and photo selection, these stories use unambiguous language and concrete visual support.

To further assist with comprehension, you may find it helpful to personalize the stories by adapting both the photographs and the text. You may add your own photographs of a child demonstrating the steps by placing them over the original photographs. The word choice may also be personalized by adding/deleting text as appropriate for each child.

Whether you use these stories as presented or whether you use them as a model to personalize, we wish you success in helping children understand these routines and gain independence!

Washing My Hands

Who: people

What: wash hands

Where: in kitchen or bathroom

When: their hands are dirty

How: by rubbing hands together with soap and water

Why: because it gets dirt and germs off hands

Hi! These are my hands.

I can do many things with my hands. I can paint, I can cover my mouth when I cough, and I can eat!

When I use my hands to paint, my hands may get paint on them. When I've finished painting, I can wash my hands. With clean hands, I can touch toys and furniture without getting paint on them!

When I use my hands to cover my mouth, my hands may get germs on them. If I'm sick, I should wash my hands throughout the day. With clean hands, I can help keep my friends and family from catching my cold!

When I use my hands to eat, my hands may get food on them. When I've finished eating, I can wash my hands. With clean hands, I can touch toys and furniture without getting food on them!

I can wash my hands in a kitchen sink or a bathroom sink. I like to wash my hands in the bathroom.

I sometimes have a hard time remembering how to wash my hands. I often forget to turn off the water! So, my mom and dad made a picture schedule to help me remember how to wash my hands. Now I can do it all by myself.

First, I turn on the water.

Then, I get my hands wet.

Next, I put some soap on my hands.

Then, I rub my hands together.

Next, I rinse off the soap.

Then, I turn off the water.

Last, I dry my hands with a towel.

Now my hands are all clean!

Things to consider when a child washes their hands

- Use of a visual schedule (print, symbols, photos) may help children with expectations and independence. Something like: turn on water, get hands wet, put soap on hands, rub hands together, rinse off soap, turn off water, dry hands with a towel, all done.

- Sensory issues such as temperature of water, texture of soap (bar, foam, liquid), and scent of soap.

- A designated washing hand song (e.g. The "Alphabet Song") or counting to a chosen number may help children rub their hands together for an appropriate time—not too long and not too short.

- Involving children in selecting their soap and/or hand towel during a shopping trip may assist with motivation.

- Use of a routine (e.g. always washing hands before or after eating) may help children remember to complete task on their own.

Getting My Hair Cut

Who: people

What: get their hair cut

Where: in salon, barber shop, or home

When: hair gets long

How: by having a stylist cut hair

Why: because a haircut keeps hair clean and looking well groomed

Today, I am going to get my hair cut.

When my hair looks or feels long, it might be time to get a haircut. It usually takes a few weeks between each haircut.

I get my hair cut at a salon. This is a place where people can get their hair cut. Other people might get their hair cut at a barber-shop or even at home.

Sometimes I have to wait for a few minutes at the salon before I get my hair cut. If I have to wait, I might read a book or sit quietly.

A person called a hairstylist cuts my hair.
Some people that cut hair are called
barbers.

When the hairstylist is ready I follow her to a chair. This is the chair I sit in while I get my hair cut.

Next, the hairstylist puts a cape on me. The cape is a piece of cloth that keeps my clothes and skin from getting hair on them.

The hairstylist uses combs, brushes, scissors, and razors to help cut my hair. There is also a mirror that lets me see how the stylist cuts my hair.

Next, the hairstylist combs my hair. Then she holds a small amount of hair and cuts it off.

As my stylist is cutting my hair, some of the hair may fall to the floor or onto the cape.

I need to sit still while I get my hair cut. This makes it easier for the stylist to cut my hair. To help me sit still the stylist might give me a small toy or a book to look at.

The stylist may need to squirt water on my
hair to get it wet. My stylist uses a squirt
bottle to get my hair wet. This makes it
easier to cut my hair.

Sometimes little pieces of hair tickle my neck or arms. The stylist will help to get them off so I feel better.

Before I get down from the chair, the stylist uses a blow dryer to blow all of the cut hair from the cape onto the floor. This helps me stay clean.

My haircut looks great!

Things to consider when a child gets a haircut

- Sensory issues such as smells of products, sensation of bits of hair on the skin, sensation of various hair cutting tools, and the sound of a blow dryer.

- Have Mom or Dad sit with the child on his or her lap during the haircut.

- Observe and visit the salon or shop before you go with your child.

- Bring a special toy or book along that will comfort your child.

- Take photos of your child completing the steps of getting a haircut (tape them into this book).

Taking My Bath

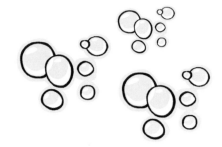

Who: children

What: take a bath

Where: in a bathtub

When: in the morning or in the evening

How: by washing their body parts with soap, and their hair with shampoo

Why: because a bath gets all the dirt, stickiness, and sweat off their bodies

During the day I may get dirty, sticky, and sweaty! I may get dirty when I help my mom make cookies. I may get sticky when I eat a lollipop. I may get sweaty when I ride my bike.

To get the dirt, stickiness, and sweat off my body, I take a bath.

When I take a bath, my dad helps me fill the bathtub with water. Tonight, my dad said I could pour soap in the water to make a bubble bath!

While the water is filling the bathtub, I take off my clothes.

When my clothes are off, I climb in the bathtub and sit down.

Before I wash, I like to play with my bath toys. My dad sets a timer for ten minutes. This lets me know how long I can play.

When the timer goes off, I need to put away my toys.

After I put away my toys, I clean my body parts. To clean my body parts, I rub soap onto a wet washcloth. Then, I rub the soapy washcloth on my face, my neck, my stomach, my arms, my legs, and my feet. My dad helps me wash my back. I rinse the soap off with water.

After I wash my body parts, I wash my hair.
First, I get my hair wet.

Next, I squeeze some shampoo onto my
hand. My dad puts a sticker on my hand to
show me how much shampoo to use. I stop
squeezing the shampoo bottle when the
sticker is covered with shampoo.

Next, I rub the shampoo all over my hair. I like to sing a song while I rub the shampoo on my hair. I stop rubbing when I finish my song.

Next, my dad helps me get the shampoo off
my hair. He does this by pouring water over
my hair eight times. I like to help him count.
It lets me know when he will stop.

When all the soap is off my hair, I stand up
and my dad pours water over my body to get
any soap off my body parts.

When all the soap is off, I climb out of the
bathtub. My body and hair are wet. I dry
them with a towel.

When I am dry, I put on my pajamas. Now I am all clean! The dirt, stickiness, and sweat are off my body.

Things to consider when a child takes a bath

- Use of a visual schedule may assist children with expectations and independence. Steps could be visually displayed using text (written explanations), symbols (line drawings), or photographs (of the child completing the task): put water in tub, take off clothes, get in tub, play, wash body, wash hair, rinse soap off, get out of tub, dry off with a towel, put clothes on, all done.

- Use of visual support may help children with independently washing their entire body: print/symbols/photos of a face, neck, stomach, arm, etc.

- Sensory issues such as temperature of water, texture of soap (bar, foam, liquid), scent of soap, texture of cleaning medium (washcloth, sponge, loofah).

- Use of tearless shampoo and soap.

- Time of day bath is given; while a bath may be calming before bedtime for some, it may be too stimulating for others.

Going to My Doctor

Who: children

What: visit a doctor

Where: at the doctor's office

When: when they are healthy and when they are sick

How: by driving to the office with their mom or dad

Why: because the doctor can make sure they are healthy and growing big and strong; if sick, a doctor may give medicine to help them get better

Today I am going to the doctor. I go to the
doctor at least once a year. He sees if I am
healthy, and he sees if I am growing big and
strong.

Sometimes, I go to the doctor when I am
sick. He may give me medicine to help me
get better.

When I get inside the doctor's office, my mom tells a lady, called a receptionist, that we are here to see the doctor.

Then, I go to the waiting room. I wait for a nurse to call my name and tell me it is my turn to see the doctor. While I wait, I like to play with the toys.

When a nurse calls my name, my mom and I walk over to her. The nurse shows us where to go and what to do.

First, the nurse tells me to take off my shoes
and stand on the scale. This lets her know
how many pounds I weigh.

Next, the nurse tells me to stand up straight against the wall. This lets her know how tall I am.

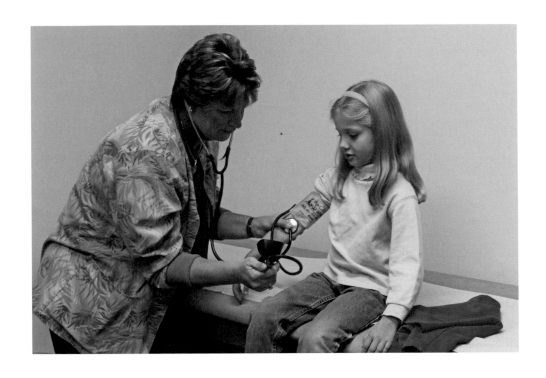

Next, the nurse takes my mom and me to a
room. She tells me to sit on the examining
table.

Then she checks my blood pressure. She
does this by wrapping a cuff around my arm
and squeezing a ball to put air in the cuff.
Checking my blood pressure lets the nurse
know how blood is moving around my body.

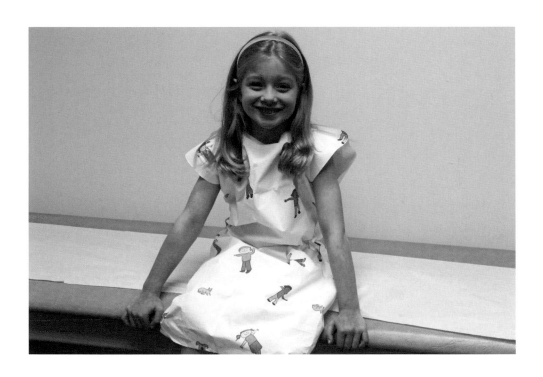

Last, the nurse tells me to put on a gown.
This makes it easier for the doctor to
examine me. After I put on the gown, I sit on
the examining table and wait for the doctor.

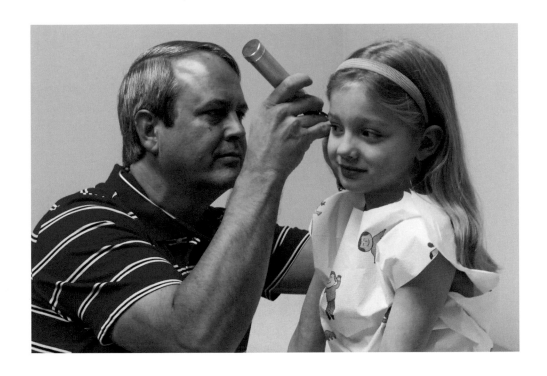

When the doctor comes in, he uses tools to look into my ears, my nose, my mouth, and my eyes. Looking into my ears, my nose, my mouth, and my eyes lets the doctor see their color and shape.

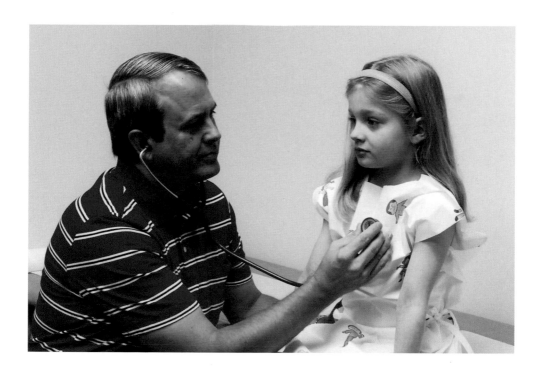

Next, the doctor listens to my heart. He does this by putting a tool called a stethoscope against my chest. Listening to my heart lets the doctor hear how it is beating.

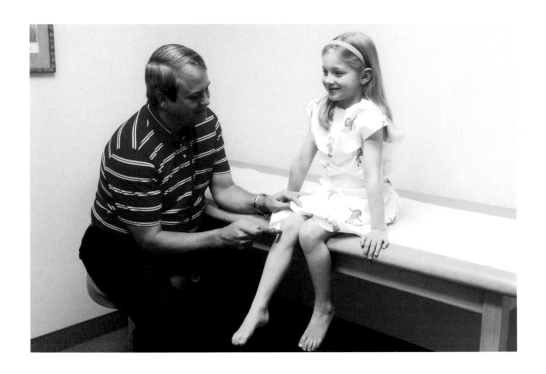

Then, the doctor checks my reflexes. He does this by gently tapping a tiny hammer below my knees. This tapping lets the doctor see if my brain is able to tell my legs to move.

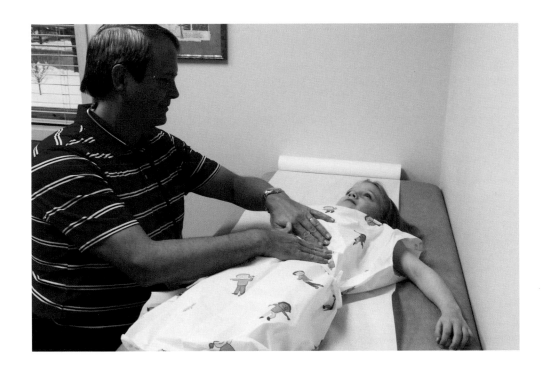

Next, the doctor tells me to lie down on the table. Then, he gently pushes on my stomach. Pushing on my stomach lets the doctor feel its size.

When the doctor has finished, he leaves the room. Then I can take off the gown and put my clothes back on.

If I need to get any shots, the nurse will come back into the room to give them to me. I don't need any shots today!

When my clothes are back on, my mom and I walk to the receptionist's desk. My mom lets the receptionist know I have finished seeing the doctor.

Now I am done! I can go outside with my mom and walk to our car.

Things to consider when a child goes to the doctor

- Prior to appointment, arrange a visit so that the child can meet his or her doctor and nurse, and can have a tour of the building and examining room.

- Take a photo of your child with his or her doctor and nurse; this may be used to familiarize the child with his or her doctor and nurse prior to the appointment.

- If the child might have an aversion or dislike for the texture of the examining gown, consider allowing him or her to choose a large t-shirt from home to bring to the appointment.

- Purchase a toy doctor's kit and engage in pretend play with the child; model actions and vocabulary from this book and allow the child to perform steps on a parent, sibling or stuffed animal.

- If waiting in the doctor's office will create significant anxiety or behavioral issues, consider calling the receptionist in the parking lot to let her know you have arrived; provide your cell number for her to call you when it is time for the child to be seen.

Brushing My Teeth

Who: people

What: brush teeth

Where: in the bathroom

When: after they eat

How: by using a toothbrush and toothpaste

Why: because it gets rid of germs caused by bits of food and keeps teeth healthy

I have learned how to take care of my teeth.

Brushing my teeth helps keep them clean and healthy.

When I was born I didn't have any teeth.My
first tooth appeared when I was a few
months old. As more teeth came through, I
learned how to brush them using a toothbrush.

My teeth help me to chew my food into smaller bits so that it is easier for me to swallow.

I usually brush my teeth after I eat a meal.
That means that I brush my teeth after
breakfast, lunch, and dinner.

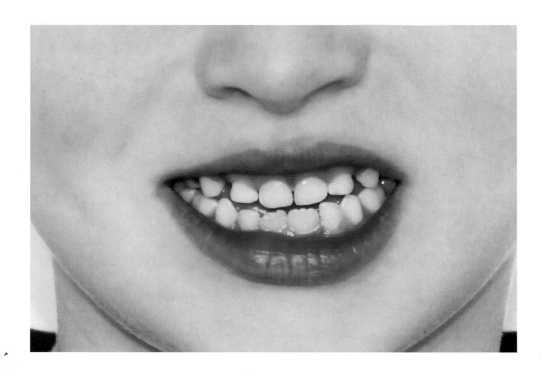

While I am eating, bits of food may get stuck between my teeth. This can cause germs. It is important to get the food items and germs off my teeth.

I have my own special toothbrush and tooth-paste, which I keep in a drawer in the bathroom.

First, I take out my toothbrush and turn on the faucet to cold water. I stick the bristles of the toothbrush under the water for a few seconds. This makes the bristles soft on my teeth when I put it in my mouth.

Next, I place my toothbrush on the counter and take out a tube of toothpaste. I gently squeeze a small amount of toothpaste onto my toothbrush. I try to squeeze out an amount that is as big as the size of a pea.

Then, I pick my toothbrush up by the handle, and carefully put the bristles in my mouth.

I begin to move the toothbrush slowly back and forth on my bottom teeth. Then I brush my top teeth until all my teeth are clean. I try to take my time when brushing my teeth. I want to make sure each tooth is clean!

When I finish brushing my teeth, I might have a lot of toothpaste in my mouth. I lean over the sink and spit the toothpaste out.

Next, I reach for a cup and turn on the cold water. I fill the cup with water. I am ready to rinse my mouth.

I take a drink of water and swish it around
the inside of my mouth. I don't swallow the
water. Instead, when I am done, I spit it into
the sink.

My teeth are clean!

Things to consider when a child brushes their teeth

- Sensory issues such as flavor of toothpaste, a gel vs. a paste, or even an electric toothbrush vs. a manual toothbrush.

- Take your child to pick out their special toothbrush and special cup.

- Use a timer, have your child sing the ABCs in their head, or listen to one song to assist with length of brushing (not too short/not too long).

- Use a chart for your child to get used to a routine; have your child place a sticker on the chart each time he/she completes the task.

- Take photographs of your child brushing his or her teeth (and tape them in this book).

of related interest

My Social Stories Book
Edited by Carol Gray and Abbie Leigh White
Illustrated by Sean McAndrew
ISBN 978 1 85302 950 9

Revealing the Hidden Social Code
Social Stories™ for People with Autistic Spectrum Disorders
Marie Howley and Eileen Arnold
Foreword by Carol Gray
ISBN 978 1 84310 222 9

Joey Goes to the Dentist
Candace Vittorini and Sara Boyer-Quick
ISBN 978 1 84310 854 2

ISPEEK at Home
Over 1300 Visual Communication Images (CD-Rom)
Janet Dixon
ISBN 978 1 84310 510 7

Do You Understand Me?
My Life, My Thoughts, My Autism Spectrum Disorder
Sofie Koborg Brøsen
ISBN 978 1 84310 464 3

Brotherly Feelings
Me, My Emotions, and My Brother with Asperger's Syndrome
Sam Frender and Robin Schiffmiller
Illustrated by Dennis Dittrich
ISBN 978 1 84310 850 4